Developing History

UNDERSTANDING AND INTERPRETING THE PAST

Ages 9-10

Jane Shuter

A & C BLACK

Contents

How can we find out about the Indus Valley civilisation?

How can we find out about the Aztecs?

What were the effects of Tudor exploration?

What can we learn about recent history by studying the life of a famous person?

Published 2007 by A & C Black Publishers Limited
38 Soho Square, London W1D 3HB
www.acblack.com

ISBN 978-0-7136-8390-5

Copyright text and illustrations © Bender Richardson White
Copyright cover illustration © Sholto Walker
Copyright photographs © Topfoto/Fotomas Index
Project managers: Lionel Bender and Ben White
Editors: Lucy Poddington and Deborah Kespert
Design: Susan McIntyre
Illustrator: Sue Woollatt
The publishers would like to thank Rick Weights and Alf Wilkinson of the Historical Association for their assistance in producing this book.

A CIP catalogue record for this book is available from the British Library.

Printed in Great Britain by Martins the Printers, Berwick on Tweed

This book is produced using paper that is made from wood grown in managed, sustainable forests. It is natural, renewable and recyclable. The logging and manufacturing processes conform to the environmental regulations of the country of origin.

Introduction

Developing History is a series of seven photocopiable activity books for history lessons. Each book provides a range of activities that not only develop children's knowledge and understanding of events, people and changes in the past, but also provide opportunities to develop their investigative and interpretive skills.

The activities vary in their approach. Some are based on first-hand observations, some present text and images for the children to analyse, and others require the children to find information from books and electronic sources. They focus on questioning, observing, generating thoughts and ideas, planning, carrying out investigations, recording findings, checking and questioning findings and presenting explanations. The activities include independent and group work.

The activities in **Developing History: Ages 9–10** are based on the QCA scheme of work for history at Key Stage 2 and support children's development in the following areas from the programme of study:
- Place events, people and changes into the correct period of time
- Use dates and vocabulary relating to the passing of time
- Understand the characteristic features of periods and societies studied, including ideas, beliefs, attitudes and experiences of men, women and children
- Social, cultural, religious and ethnic diversity of societies
- Reasons for, and results of, historical events, situations and changes
- Links between main events, situations and changes
- Recognise and give reasons for different representations and interpretations of the past
- Find out about events, people and changes from a range of sources of information, including ICT-based sources
- Ask and answer questions and select and record information relevant to the focus of the enquiry
- Recall, select and organise historical information
- Use dates and historical vocabulary to describe periods studied
- Communicate knowledge and understanding in a variety of ways.

The activities are linked with other areas of the curriculum where appropriate.

Each activity specifies the learning outcome and features a **Teachers' note** at the foot of the page, which may be masked before photocopying. This will highlight any resources needed for the activity. Expanded teaching notes are also provided in the **Notes on the activities** on pages 5–11. This section gives further information and provides key vocabulary to work through at the start of each activity.

Most of the activity sheets end with a challenge (**Now try this!**) which reinforces and extends the children's learning and provides the teacher with an opportunity for assessment. These activities might be appropriate for only a few children; it is not expected that the whole class should complete them.

Organisation and resources

Most activities require few resources beyond pencils and general classroom items, including spare paper on occasion. However, because the programme of study for history requires the use of primary source materials and the examination of objects from the time being studied (not just drawings of these objects), there will be times when children will need additional resources. They may need to have access to books, CD-ROMs, DVDs or to computers to search the Internet for images and information. These occasions will be pointed out in the **Teachers' note**. You may also want to use an interactive whiteboard or an overhead projector to display the activity sheets or source material.

Ensure you have a simple class timeline to help the children place the period in its chronological context. The timeline helps them to meet the requirements to place events, people and changes into the correct periods of time and to use dates and vocabulary related to the passing of time. Clearly mark the direction in which to move along the timeline. The timeline needs to have AD and BC (and the direction in which these move along the timeline) clearly marked. It would also be useful to have a chart on the wall that shows how pre-decimal coinage worked. You will find it helpful to build up your own resource bank of books (including picture books and story books about the various study units), posters, newspapers and old photographs, especially of your local area or historic sites you and your class could visit.

Structure of a history lesson

To get the best use of the activity sheets, gather all the resources you need before the lesson. Spend 10 to 15 minutes discussing the activity and making sure all the children understand what they have to do and how they will achieve it. Give the children about 20 minutes on the activity. Allow 5 to 10 minutes for whole-class review and consolidation.

Useful websites

You can find information and pictures relating to the topics in this book on the following websites:
www.barnardos.org.uk
www.victorianweb.org
(This site is more useful for your research than for the children, but it has a wealth of information)
www.learningcurve.gov.uk
www.makingthemodernworld.org.uk/stories/the_age_of_the_engineer
www.primaryresources.co.uk/history
www.spartacus.schoolnet.co.uk

Notes on the activities

The notes below expand upon those provided at the foot of the activity pages. They give ideas for making the most of the activity sheet, including suggestions for the whole-class introduction and discussion or for follow-up work. To help teachers to select appropriate learning experiences for their pupils, the activities are grouped into sections within each book, but the pages need not be presented in the order in which they appear unless stated otherwise.

What was it like for children living in Victorian Britain?

Resources • Unit 11

Timeline – Pictures of Queen Victoria in 1838 and 1897. Examples can be found at
http://www.wga.hu/frames-e.html?/html/s/sully/index.html
www.bbc.co.uk/history/ancient/vikings/revival_02.shtml
Different lives – books, CD-ROMs and the Internet to research a rich girl's Sunday
Changing children's lives – books, CD-ROMs and the Internet to research the life of Thomas Barnardo
Happy holidays – books, CD-ROMs and the Internet to research hop picking and seaside holidays
Picture the past – paintings and photos of the seaside in Victorian times. There are a wide range of sources for this. The best images are probably still in books, which you should be able to find in the 'art and photography' section of your local library. Look for 'genre' paintings, which purport to show everyday life in Victorian times. Many local libraries also have useful photographic collections. One of the best seaside paintings with a wealth of detail for examination and comparison is W.P. Frith's *Life at the Seaside (Ramsgate Sands)*. It is reprinted in many books and used on websites. You can find it in the Royal Collection and on its website. The painting is also available as a large poster. It is a useful resource for talking about holidays, childhood and class.

Then and now (page 12) considers the different attitudes to children and work in modern and Victorian times. Discuss what the children want to be when they grow up. Write four of their chosen jobs on the board. Talk about how they will train for each one. Pick three examples that require a training course, not just learning on the job. Then look at how the Victorians thought children should learn a job. In Victorian times, education was not widely seen as valuable until the end of the period. Today, education is seen as a necessary stepping stone to employment. As a follow-up, children can discuss how Victorian sayings, such as 'children should be seen and not heard', would be thought of now, and if children would conform to them.

Different lives (page 13) encourages children to consider how not all children in Victorian Britain, even sometimes those in the same household, had the same kinds of lives. Begin by discussing the Victorian class system. Then explain that they are going to read about the lives of two Victorian girls of the same age in the same house and from the same year. Do the **Now try this!** activity

as a whole-class exercise to provoke empathy. Encourage more than a knee-jerk reaction such as, 'Jane would be envious' or 'Julia would be horrified'. Julia might well see nothing wrong with Jane's day. That's what working-class girls did. Jane might think that Julia couldn't look after herself and was too much of a baby.

Changing children's lives (page 14) allows the children the opportunity for research work and organising biographical information. It aims to bring them to an understanding of how individuals can affect society. Begin by giving a brief biographical outline of Dr Barnardo's life. Visit www.barnardos.org.uk for information. The children researching what Barnardos does today should visit the 'What we do' section of the same website. They can find out what systems are in place to help orphans now. This ties in with Citizenship.

Caught (page 15) Begin by reminding the children of work they have done on the Education Acts or by outlining the main provisions of the most important Acts. The 1870 Education Act provided the first state schools and gave the Boards of Education the right to make education between the ages of 5–13 compulsory in their area. Compulsory education for children aged 5–10 was not introduced across the country until 1880 and was not free until 1891. Remind the class that children from poorer families went out to work from as young as eight years old. In farming communities, they started at an even earlier age. These families resented compulsory education because they lost income if their children went to school. They also had to pay school fees until 1890. Once education was compulsory, the police and school inspectors made sure that all children went to school. Before starting the activity, explain that the children will be looking at a primary source from a Victorian newspaper. For extension work, split the class into four groups and give out 'family description' sheets based on the information below. Then hold a debate on compulsory education.
Family one: father who is a train driver; mother at home; young baby; two boys aged six and five.
Family two: father and mother who are out of work; young baby; two girls aged six and eight who work at a factory; one girl aged four.
Family three: father and mother who are both farm workers; four children aged ten, eight, five and three; twins aged six. The eldest girl minds the children. The eldest boy works on the farm.
Family four: father who is a shopkeeper; mother, who works in the shop; one boy aged six; one girl aged seven.

All change (page 16) encourages the children to look for similarities and differences between two primary sources showing cloth making. Remind them of any work they have done previously on the domestic system or factories, or briefly introduce these topics. The first picture, from 1742, shows the domestic system that was in place before the rise of the factories. Under the domestic system, the employer delivered wool for workers to spin and weave at home. Women worked in their own time, around household tasks and childcare. The second picture shows the factory system. This activity can be conducted as a two-stage, whole-class discussion, filling in the chart in between discussions.

> **Vocabulary:** *factory, machinery, supervisor.*

Happy holidays (page 17) gives children a chance to do some research on holidays. It would be useful to have images of Victorian holidays on display. First, discuss how holidays developed in the Victorian period. The amount of time you spend on this will depend on how much you have covered the topic previously. It was not until the late Victorian period that anyone but the upper classes went on holiday regularly. However, from the mid-Victorian period onwards, holidays were a feature of middle-class life and even working-class people, due to changes in the law about working hours, got one week off a year. Holidays by the seaside were especially popular for the 'good air'. Working-class people in the south of England, especially Londoners, often went to work in Kent for a week picking fruit or hops. The job was hard and the living conditions basic, but they were in the countryside and saw it as a holiday.

> **Vocabulary:** *hop-picking, pier, promenade, seaside.*

Picture the past (page 18) looks at paintings and photographs as sources. Begin by discussing how the details of a painting or photo can give us lots of information. Display a modern example on the board and brainstorm what it tells you about items such as clothes, buildings, equipment. Also look at how any people depicted are feeling. You can repeat the exercise with W.P. Frith's 'The Railway Station', which he painted using photographs of Paddington Station in London. This has huge amounts of information about Victorian clothing, luggage, railway station architecture and train design. It even shows that people put luggage on the roof. This is a useful painting to keep on display for discussing many aspects of the period. It is reproduced in many textbooks and can also be found at: http://www.spartacus.schoolnet.co.uk/RAfrith.htm

> **Vocabulary:** *painting, photograph, seaside, interpretation.*

Different homes (page 19) encourages children to understand that the Victorian period, and indeed any period, can be viewed quite differently depending on the evidence available. Situations can also be viewed differently depending on whose perspective or viewpoint you are considering. The water piped to the houses of the rich sometimes came from reservoirs or rivers in the countryside around London. It was often still dirty water from the River Thames. However, it was piped into tanks and the filth settled at the bottom. This meant it was cleaner than taking water straight from the river. As a follow-up activity, the children can discuss how they think Clara and Henry would react to visiting each other's houses. They can also discuss modern water supplies, health and hygiene. Using books and the Internet, they can find out about diseases carried by water and how these affect people in parts of the world where the water is not purified or treated.

> **Vocabulary:** *cholera, drain, sewer.*

How did life change in Victorian times?

Resources • Unit 12

- This unit focuses on local history. The resources offered by record offices and local libraries vary widely. Consult the local record office or your History advisor about the material available in your area and the easiest way to access it. They may also know of websites by local history groups.
- **Using the census** – copies of census data for a local street. You can choose to provide the children with copies of the pages or with transcripts. Some census recorders had handwriting that was easy to read, others presented more of a challenge! Assess what best suits the children
- **Full steam ahead** – a Victorian map of the area showing the nearest railway line
- **Let's go shopping** – at least two photos of the main shopping street in your nearest town from the beginning and the end of the Victorian period. More photos would be even better. You need these to see how the street has changed. Trade directories for the street are also useful
- **Changing places** – illustrations of typical Victorian houses.

Using the census (page 20) makes use of the 1851 census, not the first census from 1841, which only recorded name, age, birth year and relationship to the head of the household. The 1851 census includes occupation, gender, marital status and birthplace, so it tells you more. Begin by making sure the children understand the words 'census', 'household' and 'occupation'. Explain why you are not using the first census and discuss why the additional information is so useful. Encourage the children to think of their own questions that might appear on the census. Read through the census data together.

> **Vocabulary:** *census, household, occupation, street directory, trade directory.*

Full steam ahead (page 21) shows the rapid expansion of the railways in early Victorian times. Base the activity on your local area. Begin by brainstorming why the railways expanded so fast. The amount of information you give to the children will depend on the amount of work done previously on the topic. One reason for expansion is that the technology was there to make the trains and build the lines. Another was that increasing industrialisation and urbanisation meant people travelled more and goods needed to be shifted. As a follow-up activity, have a class discussion on the unplanned effects of this expansion. These include the use of the railways for leisure and the standardisation of time across the country.

> **Vocabulary:** *canal, industrialisation, railway, transport, urbanisation.*

All aboard (page 22) encourages the children to consider how the class system ran through all aspects of Victorian life, even the newly-invented railways. End the lesson with a class discussion about which carriages various people would occupy, for example a factory worker, a mine owner, a housemaid and a doctor. Where would a governess travel with the children she is in charge of? Ask the children for their views on the class system today, including on the railways.

> **Vocabulary:** *middle class, upper class, working class.*

Let's go shopping (page 23) requires at least two photos of a main street in a big town, preferably local to your area. One of the photos should be from the 1890s and the other from as early as possible in the Victorian period. Depending on the resources available, more photos for the intervening years would be useful. Children should be encouraged to look at the kinds of shops in the street and whether they have changed by the end of the period. Depending on the amount of work they have done on Victorian shops, they may need some help with the names of small specialist shops.

> **Vocabulary:** *barber, fishmonger, greengrocer, ironmonger.*

Changing places (page 24) focuses on changes in the Victorian period. The **Now try this!** encourages the children to continue the comparison into modern times. Begin the activity by discussing how things change and how those changes affect the way people live. Talk about this in terms of the future. If people in the future have cheap, fast space travel, how will this affect where they choose to live and work? The changes the children need to find are: the postbox for quicker reliable communication; the train and bus for travelling faster, and working and buying food further from home; the bicycle for quicker personal transport; the paving and gas lighting for improved public services.

> **Vocabulary:** *change, commuting, services.*

How has life in Britain changed since 1948?

Resources • Unit 13
  Going decimal – a currency conversion chart for display
  Clean and dry – books and the Internet to investigate doing the laundry since 1948
  Going to Butlins – access to www.butlinsmemories.co.uk or material taken from this site, modern Butlins brochures.

Keep in touch (page 25) encourages the children to consider how ways of communicating have expanded, and the effects this has had on our lives. Begin by making sure the children are familiar with all the communication methods described. The table can be completed as a whole-class exercise. As a follow-up, discuss how the immediacy of email and mobile phones means that people now expect to get in touch with each other instantly. For example, when meeting friends, there is no need to make detailed arrangements beforehand in case you miss the bus. Indeed, people do not even need a prearranged meeting place. Link this to Citizenship with a debate about at what age you should be allowed to own a mobile phone.

> **Vocabulary:** *email, letter, mobile phone, telephone, telegram.*

Going decimal (page 26) focuses on a major change in Britain. Begin by discussing the change in currency with the children and working through the conversion chart. End the session with a discussion of why many people objected to the new currency, even though it was easier to use. What were their reasons? You might also discuss what impact introducing the euro to Britain might have. The activity links with numeracy.

> **Vocabulary:** *pence, pound, shilling .*

Clean and dry (page 27) provides the children with a chance to show how doing the washing has changed in the UK since the 1940s. The activity can be done as a whole-class exercise, with enlarged copies of the pictures from the sheet to peg onto a class timeline. Follow up with a discussion about the length of time it took to wash clothes in the copper, then wring them in the mangle and dry them. Remember that clothes were dried in front of the fire if it was raining outside. Brainstorm words for how a wet wash day would make the person washing feel.

> **Vocabulary:** *automatic washing machine, copper, mangle, spin drier, tumble drier, twin tub, washing line.*

Going to Butlins (page 28) allows the children to chart yet another change from the 1940s, this time the changing face of one holiday camp. Children will need access to the website www.butlinsmemories.co.uk or to material that you have taken from this site for them to use. They can also use Butlins' holiday brochures, although these will only help them to find out about modern-day holidays at Butlins.

> **Vocabulary:** *abroad, brochure, holiday, holiday camp.*

A person's history (page 29) encourages the children to consider the usefulness of oral history and the kinds of questions to ask in an interview. Begin by making sure they understand what oral history is. Go on to discuss appropriate questions, such as 'What was it like when you were at school?' Discuss questions that would not be appropriate as well, for example, 'What happened on 10 December 1953?' As a follow-up, the children should brainstorm areas of life that make good subjects for personal memories, such as school days. Then they should draw up a list of questions for one topic. They could go on to interview a family member for homework about this topic.

> **Vocabulary:** *interview, interviewee, interviewer.*

Evidence (page 30) allows the children to identify different items as being characteristic of a particular decade. Begin by discussing each piece of evidence. Stress that everything is evidence to a historian. Pick up a couple of things from your desk and ask how they are evidence of school life today. Explain that the artefacts on the activity sheet have been chosen because they belong to a particular decade. The activity is suitable for whole-class work, with the children debating which decade each item belongs to and individuals fixing a label for that item onto the timeline. As a follow-up activity, discuss what each item tells them about other aspects of life. For example the ration book shows there were still food shortages and that rationing would have made cooking a problem.

> **Vocabulary:** *afghan coat, decade, LP, ration book, Sega Megadrive, Walkman.*

Who were the ancient Greeks?

Resources • Unit 14
- General map to show ancient Greece and the city states. An online map can be found at www.bartleby.com/67/aeolia01.html
- **Powerful gods** – books, CD-ROM and the Internet to research the relationships between the gods of Olympus
- **Olympic Games** – a clear image of at least one Greek vase

with an Olympic event on it from books or the Internet. The best place to find clear images on the web that do not offend the sensibilities (people competed naked) is the Bridgeman Art Library at http://www.bridgeman.co.uk Search for charioteers [BAL 28560 or CZA 228737], boxers [BAT 99068], foot racers [DTR 114497 or XIR 158663] and discus and javelin throwers [BAL 110798].

Greek women (page 31) allows children to identify the differences in attitude to women between the city states of Athens and Sparta. Begin by reminding them, with reference to a map, of the way Greece was divided up into city states. Also remind them that the city states were not ruled in the same way. You could consider the government of various city states as an extension to the activity: the BBC website on ancient Greece has a good section on government, which would provide a lead in to the next activity on Democracy: www.bbc.co.uk/schools/ancientgreece/corinth/govt.shtml

> **Vocabulary:** *Athens, barracks, city, state, Sparta, warrior.*

Democracy (page 32) encourages children to consider the features of democracy and other systems of government. If you did not use the BBC website for the previous activity, consider using it now. The amount of introductory discussion needed will depend on the work the children have done previously. You can extend the activity by comparing ancient Greek and modern democracy. This links to Citizenship.

> **Vocabulary:** *citizen, democracy, government, slave.*

Powerful gods (page 33) gives the children a chance to sort out the 12 major deities of Greece who were supposed to live on Mount Olympus. Remember, it is difficult for modern children to empathise with people who believed that the gods could influence their lives directly if they did not behave properly and make sacrifices. So begin with a class discussion about this point. For a follow-up activity, discuss Greek myths and legends. A myth centres on the gods; a legend often involves the gods, but focuses on a hero. The children should then write a modern-day story where one of the gods they have discussed comes to Earth and influences daily life.

> **Vocabulary:** *god, goddess, prayer.*

Towering temples (page 34) enables the children to get to grips with temple architecture. Greek temples varied in size, but followed a similar pattern. Talk this pattern through using the vocabulary in the word bank. Temples usually ran east to west with a central naos (where the statue of the god was kept), which had walls around it. The front wall, which faced the altar in the east, had a door in it so the god could 'see' sacrifices. There were two half-walled porches at the front and the back. All around this was an area with columns and three steps down to ground level. The questions aim at drawing out the difference between mud-brick houses built for mortal humans and stone built temples built for the immortal gods. The **Now try this!** asks children to think of points the Greeks would have made such as 'it will please the gods', 'the gods will then be more likely to favour the temple-builders', 'it will show the city state is rich and has good, religious people in it'.

> **Vocabulary:** *altar, back porch, front porch, naos, temple.*

Solve Sparta's problem (page 35) encourages children to empathise with the Spartans over the Athenian request that they hurry to Marathon to fight the Persians. Begin by discussing the situation the Spartans faced. It is summarised at the start of the activity sheet. The Persians invaded Greece in 494 BC (point out Marathon on the class map). They were angry with the Athenians for helping other city states rebel against Persian control. The Athenians asked the Spartans for help to fight the Persians, who had about 20,000 soldiers. The Athenians had about 10,000. However, the Spartans were in the middle of a 15-day religious festival. The Spartans would all have had their own ideas about what to do depending on the strength of their religious beliefs and their sense of honour. However, they had to do what their king decided.

> **Vocabulary:** *city, Marathon, Persians, religious festival, state, warrior.*

Wonderful warriors (page 36) introduces children to the phalanx, the battle formation that made Greek warriors so successful. Begin by discussing how important it is for people in battle to work together and support each other. Then read the sources together. The **Now try this!** asks the children to experiment with biased and unbiased writing. You could do this as a whole-class exercise. Discuss the emotive language used by the Greek speaker and how there are often emotive adjectives in biased writing when you discuss the sources.

> **Vocabulary:** *armour, hoplite, phalanx, tactics, warrior, weapons.*

Olympic Games (page 37) is about the Olympics but it is also about using sources. Before beginning the activity, remind the children about the difference between primary and secondary sources and explain that secondary sources can be just as valuable (and reliable) as primary sources. Both can be accurate and unbiased, both can be inaccurate and biased. We need to know where they come from to judge this.

> **Vocabulary:** *stadium, primary source, secondary source.*

How do we use ancient Greek ideas today?

Resources • Unit 15
- **Greek style** – picture of a Greek temple. Many books have these, or try the Bridgeman Art Library website http://www.bridgeman.co.uk and search for BAL 124240
- **Greek thinkers** – books, CD-ROM and the Internet.

Easy as ABC (page 38) encourages the children to compare our alphabet with the ancient Greek alphabet and look for similarities and differences. Introduce the activity by writing the first few letters of the alphabet on the board, then stop and ask what you are writing out. When you get the answer 'alphabet', explain that this word comes from the first two letters of the ancient Greek alphabet, alpha and beta. Tell the children that the Greek language has influenced the English language and many English words come from Greek words. Then look at the two alphabets. As an extension, talk about the fact that an alphabet is a tool for writing down what is said, so it reflects the spoken word. The differences between the two alphabets can be tied to the different sounds used in the two languages. Work through the sounds for each letter. You can refer to the following website; www.ibiblio.org/koine/greek/lessons/alphabet.html. This site also gives the Greek alphabet in order. The children could then try, by sound, to put their names into ancient Greek.

> **Vocabulary:** *alphabet, language.*

School time (page 39) requires the children to compare modern and Athenian school practices. Begin the activity by reminding the children about the different ideas that different city states had about government and education. This exercise refers to schools in Athens. Spartan boys were entirely focussed on becoming warriors. Only boys had any formal education. Girls were expected to marry and have children. Many Greek women were educated but learned by asking older brothers or other relatives to teach them. Reasons for differences to today include smaller schools because there were no girls; a smaller population; the teacher could decide on the number of pupils ; there was no 'working week' or holiday-time even though religion was important; slaves no longer existed; and all schools were fee-paying so pupils were given more privileges.

> **Vocabulary:** *poetry, lessons, term, memorise, supervise.*

Greek style (page 40) Begin the activity by remind the children what they have learned about Greek temples and display pictures. if you do not have any, visit Bridgeman Art Library website www.bridgeman.co.uk and search for BAL 124240. Greek architecture has influenced later periods. Use examples of local Victorian architecture with Greek features to illustrate this point.

> **Vocabulary:** *column, entablature (the stonework between the columns and the pediment/roof), pediment (the triangular pieces at the top front and back, often filled with carved friezes), temple.*

Greek thinkers (page 41) The cards here support a research activity such as that suggested in the QCA schemes of work for this unit. Begin by brainstorming as many school subjects as the children can think of. Then explain that the basic ideas used in many of these subjects come from ancient Greek thinkers.

> **Vocabulary:** *politics, history, geography, mathematics.*

Olympics: 1 & **2** (pages 42 & 43) focus on the similarities and differences between the modern and ancient Olympics. There are few similarities: the mainly amateur status of the competitors and the four year gap between Olympics events. There are many differences. As well as those conveyed on page 42 , the children should consider that all ancient Olympic competitors were Greek and that wars were stopped so that people could travel to the Games.

> **Vocabulary:** *amateur, city, competitor, event, religious festival, professional, spectator, state.*

How can we find out about the Indus Valley civilisation?

Resources • Unit 16(a)
- **Timeline** – Begin this unit by finding the dates for the Indus Valley civilisation (3500–2500 BC) and fixing them on the

timeline. Stress that these dates are approximate and, remind the children about AD and BC dating. A map that shows the area settled by the Indus Valley people would be useful, too.
- **Interpreting evidence** – photographs of an Indus Valley artefact. These can be found in reference books, on history CD-ROMs and on photo library sites on the Internet. Go to website www.bbc.co.uk/schools/indusvalley/ and follow the links to the artefacts or try www.harappa.com

Archaeological evidence (page 44) introduces children to the idea of historical conclusions being tentative, based on best guesses using the available evidence. Depending on how much work you have done on evidence before, you could produce a modern artefact, such as a plastic toy duck, and discuss with the children what it tells them. Ask what it is made of, whether it looks hand-made, who might have made it, what it could be used for (putting in water, plastic is waterproof), and who it could be for. The most likely conclusion is that it is a bath toy for a child. But what would an archaeologist from the future think of it? The archaeologist is likely to reach the same conclusion about materials but might have a different idea about use, for example an offering to put in the pond of a water god. Begin the activity by reminding the children that we cannot yet read Indus Valley writing, so non-written evidence is vital.

> **Vocabulary:** *archaeologist, artefact, excavate.*

Indus Valley homes (page 45) encourages the children to draw conclusion from artwork drawn from archaeological evidence. Remind the children that there are usually two levels of information to be derived from evidence: the facts and the inferences.

> **Vocabulary:** *drain, well.*

Interpreting evidence (page 46) follows the activities on pages 44 and 45, so the children need not be reminded about facts and inferences. Explain that they are going to do more evidence work, this time with a photograph of an artefact. Stress that they need to examine the artefact closely and think about it carefully to answer the questions. This activity is designed for use with Unit 16b (Aztecs) as well.

> **Vocabulary:** *artefact, inference, evidence.*

Take a close look (page 47) uses detailed drawings of an artefact. Drawings of an artefact are useful, even if they are one step removed from the artefact itself. They can be more or less useful depending on the circumstances in which they were made. For example, were they made using the artefact or a photo for reference. Or were they from memory? Consider the care taken and the purpose of the drawing. Was it a quick sketch as a memento or a detailed copy for historical study?

> **Vocabulary:** *artefact.*

How can we find out about the Aztecs?

Resources • Unit 16(b)
- **Timeline** – begin this unit by finding the dates for the Aztec civilisation (AD 1200–1520) and fixing them on the timeline. Remind the children about AD and BC dating. A map

showing the area controlled by the Aztecs would be useful.

- **Floating farmland** – books, CD-ROMs and the Internet to research the modern chinampas of Mexico City. For the **Now try this!**, you will find useful information at www.transitionsabroad.com/publications/magazine/0411/ xochimilco_gardens_in_mexico_city.shtml
- **A splendid city** – a photo of the whole of the Acropolis. If you do not already have one, visit http://pro.corbis.com and search for image YA011228

Floating farmland (page 48) Begin by reminding the children that the Aztecs came to live on Lake Texcoco because they were driven out of other places by enemy tribes. Their first homes were reed huts on a small rocky island in the lake. They expanded the city by filling in the swampy areas around the island with rocks, rubbish and the marshy mud dug out of the lake. By carefully managing the filling in and digging out, they made areas of firm land and canals to move around. They needed to grow food, so made floating farmland, or chinampas. To do this, they marked out long, thin rectangles in the swamp using poles and reed mats. Layers of reeds, branches and stones were built up in the mat 'bed' until there was a solid surface just above the water level. Then they covered this in mud from the bottom of the lake to make fertile soil for crops.

Vocabulary: *canals, chinampa(s), crops.*

A splendid city (page 49) uses an engraving of an impression of the Tenochtitlan's central square in Aztec times. It was in the middle of Lake Texcoco and about 500 m sq. The children may ask how something this heavy could have been built on a lake! Remind them that the main part of Tenochtitlan was constructed on a rocky island in the middle of the lake and it was the first place the Aztecs built. They had about 1.5 sq km of solid land (the size of almost 5,000 tennis courts) to work with before they needed to build chinampas. The swampy land around the island was the easiest to reclaim as further out, the water deepened. For the **Now try this!** section, similarities to the Acropolis include that it was situated in the central part of the city; built from stone, had a large temple for religious ceremonies (showing the importance of religion to both civilisations); the important part of the temple was small and hard to get to; and the area was walled. Differences are that the Acropolis was built high above the city; it had no ball court or school; and the temple's shape was different (not a pyramid).

Vocabulary: *ball court, island, religious ceremony, paving, plaza, temple.*

Different views (page 50) allows the children to explore the idea that different people can have different views of the same situation. Depending on how much work the children have done on this topic previously, you might want to introduce the idea by discussing a modern example. Why would the supporters of two different football teams have different views about whether they had watched a 'good' match between their teams if one side won five goals to nil?

Vocabulary: *cannons, coward, interpret, peace.*

Take a closer look (page 51) uses copies of actual Aztec drawings. Representations or artist's impressions of ancient drawings are useful, even if they are one step removed from the drawings themselves. They can be more or less useful depending on the circumstances in which they were made. For example, were they made using the artefact or a photo for reference. Or were they from memory? Consider the care taken and the purpose of the drawing. Was it a quick sketch as a memento or a detailed copy for historical study?

Vocabulary: *artefact, representation. interpretation.*

What were the effects of Tudor exploration?

Resources • Unit 19
- **Timeline** – Begin this unit by reminding the children about the dates of Tudor rule and fixing them on the timeline. Make sure the children understand about AD and BC dating.
- **Tudor world view** – modern atlases
- **Round the world: 1 and 2** – modern atlases

Tudor world view (page 52) helps children to realise how much of the world they know was discovered in the Tudor period (and not all by explorers from the UK). Begin the lesson by emphasising how little of the world people knew about in 1480. Explain that there were few maps and that explorers often came back with strange and frightening stories, so they must have been very curious and brave. Remind the children of the work they have done on exploration so far, for example Spain, Portugal and New World gold, and of the fact that different countries competed to find and claim new lands and their resources. Many explorers were looking for a route to China by sea to avoid the expensive, difficult and dangerous overland journey for trading silks and spices.

Vocabulary: *expedition, explorer, Europe, spices.*

Life on board (page 53) emphasises the physical discomfort of life on board ship. Tudor sailors slept in the hold, on the softer stores, like rope and sails, or on the deck. Hammocks were not in use until 1596. The sailors did not wash, even though they were often soaked by storms, and they went to the toilet over the side of the ship. This activity can be extended by discussing what the cabin boy might have been dreading about the voyage. Was he scared of sea monsters? How did he feel about sleeping in the hold, rough seas, going to the toilet over the side of the ship, attacks by pirates or getting lost?

Vocabulary: *deck, hold, lice, hammock.*

Dangerous voyages (page 54) focuses on the perils of navigation. Remind the children that explorers often did not have maps to follow, only stories from other sailors and sometimes not even that. The navigational instruments were better than those of previous centuries, but they still seem very rudimentary to us. There was no satellite navigation, radar, sonar and few accurate charts or maps.

Vocabulary: *chart, course, reef, navigate.*

Round the world: 1 & 2 (pages 55 and 56) give the children practice of sorting the events of Drake's voyage around the world chronologically. Remind them that Portugal and Spain were hostile to England at this time, although not actually at war. So Drake was sailing in hostile waters for much of the time Drake was a privateer. This means he attacked 'enemy' ships and gave a share of the treasures to Queen Elizabeth. The Spanish and Portuguese ships sailing from South America were full of gold, silver and pearls. This made them especially valuable prizes. The Spanish and Portuguese guarded the ships in the Atlantic and fortified their towns. On the Pacific side of South America, towns and ships were much less well guarded.

> **Vocabulary:** *privateer, prize.*

Viewpoints (page 57) Begin by reminding the children of their work on different viewpoints. Explain that, during their voyages, the *Elizabeth* and the *Golden Hind* both had to be put into shore to fetch fresh water and for repair. The quotation from Francis Fletcher's account of his voyage is a primary source, edited for difficult language.

> **Vocabulary:** *chaplain, bias.*

Different lives (page 58) shows a black and white copy of a colour drawing made by John White. White was on the 1585 expedition to Virginia. He went along to illustrate a book, published in 1590, about the people, animals and plants of Virginia. The book was written by Thomas Harriot, who was on the 1585 expedition. Begin by telling the children that historians think White's drawings of the plants and animals of the New World were very accurate. Therefore the drawing gives us a good indication of what an Indian village was like at the time. The things we know from the drawing are that the villagers had a fence of poles, made their houses with woven mats over a wooden frame, had boards along the sides of the houses and had a big fire outside. Examples of what we might infer are that the fire was to keep animals or other people out, that they may have built the houses as a group, that they slept, sat and stored things on the boards, that they may or may not have had fires inside the buildings. The houses are high enough to not be too smoky but all the construction material is flammable.

> **Vocabulary:** *board, frame, mat, woven.*

Exploration impact (page 59) is intended for use at the end of the unit, to get the children to summarise what they have learned about exploration. Begin by explaining that what we do, even small things, have effects. Not all of these effects are intended. You might open a window. An intentional effect would be deciding to let fresh air into the room to wake people up. An unintentional effect would be a gust of wind blowing over a display. The children should think about the intentional and unintentional effects of exploration.

> **Vocabulary:** *discovery, impact.*

What can we learn about recent history by studying the life of a famous person?

Resources • Unit 20
- **Bob Geldof** – books, CD-ROMs and the Internet
- **More aid** – books, CD-ROMs and the Internet to research Live Aid, Sport Aid (Run the World), Band Aid II, Live 8 and Band Aid 20

Bob Geldof (page 60) gives the children a chance to research the life of Bob Geldof. Explain that they are studying him because he has had a direct impact on events and the lives of many people. He also reflects concerns of his time such as poverty and aid. However, the research materials need to be chosen carefully avoiding adult content and language. The Wikipedia website entry http://en.wikipedia.org/wiki/Bob_Geldof is accurate and of a reasonable reading level. Children can explore this freely. www.commissionforafrica.org/english/commissioners/bios/geldof.html is a good site and Bob Geldof's official website www.bobgeldof.info is useful for his music and charity work. Follow the links to 'Charity' and 'Band Aid' for a synopsis of band Aid's formation. Bob Geldof was born 5 October 1951, near Dublin, Ireland. He went to a Catholic school and left at sixteen. He worked in a slaughterhouse, as a road builder and in a vegetable canning factory, then he travelled to Canada to work as a music journalist for a newspaper in Vancouver.

> **Vocabulary:** *Band Aid, poverty, charity.*

Band Aid (page 61) introduces the children to Band Aid and asks them to explore reasons celebrities have for doing charity work. The original Band Aid worked so well because Bob Geldof had contacts in the music world and he could use his celebrity status to publicise the record. Also, he was prepared to stand up to the government when it wanted to keep the VAT tax on the records. It is important to underline that Bob Geldof's success does not mean that charities like Oxfam were not working. They all work on a global scale. However, they had set ways of working. One of Band Aid's big effects on charity work is that it showed you could cut out red tape to get aid to a particular place fast.

> **Vocabulary:** *band aid (sticking plaster), single.*

Making things happen (page 62) asks the children to compare two different kinds of sources. Remind them that different kinds of sources tell you different things. A diary entry or a letter might tell you about a person's feelings. A book of accounts tells you if a shopkeeper is making money or not. Link this to literacy. As an extension activity, discuss how the sources are also sources about Bob Geldof. The quotation is a primary source (Geldof himself) and shows his passionate commitment to the people of Africa. The statistics are secondary information. They show the success of his project.

> **Vocabulary:** *food, livelihood, security, source, statistics, primary, secondary.*

More aid (page 63) asks children to do more research into Geldof's further involvement in charity work. Their research will show how the scale of the Band Aid Charitable Trust's work has widened from one record to concerts, charity runs and more political involvement such as the G8 summit.

> **Vocabulary:** *sanitation, sorghum, trust.*

Changing people (page 64) aims at getting the children to summarise how they feel Bob Geldof changed people's view of giving to charity. The children will form their own opinions through studying history. They need to explain why they think as they do and provide supporting arguments and evidence.

> **Vocabulary:** *argument, evidence.*

Then and now

Understand how attitudes to children changed over time

Henry and Mary were Victorian children.

James and Emma are alive today.

- **Draw lines to link each child to the right speech bubble.**

I'm six. I go to school and will do until I'm 18. My dad says an education is important. I help on the farm in my spare time.

I'm six. I work in the field, picking up stones. My Dad says farm workers start learning early!

I'm ten. I want to be a nanny. I'll need to get GCSEs and train as a nanny first. I won't work with children until I'm about 18.

I'm ten. I'm a nursery maid. Nanny's teaching me what to do. When I'm older, I'll be a nanny.

| Henry | Mary | James | Emma |

How have ideas about learning a job changed?

- **Write your explanation.**

_____

_____

_____

Why do think Victorian children were made to start work so young?

- **Write your ideas with a partner.**

Teachers' note Allow time for a preliminary discussion. Remind the children what the words 'nursery maid' and 'nanny' mean before they start the activity. Nannies were in charge of the nursery. They taught nursery maids their job. Compare attitudes to children and work between Victorian times and today. The speech bubbles match the children from the left as follows: James, Henry, Emma, Mary.

Developing History
Age 9-10
© **A & C BLACK**

Different lives

Understand that ways of life differed greatly across Victorian society

Julia was the daughter of a rich Victorian business man. Jane was a servant in his house.

Jane

Julia

I get up at 7.30 am, when Nanny brings me and my sisters hot water to wash.

Nanny helps us dress. Breakfast is in the nursery at 8.30 am. After that, we have lessons with the governess in the schoolroom until lunch in the nursery at 1 pm. Then we go for a walk in the garden and play until teatime at 5 pm. After tea, we go downstairs to see our parents for an hour, if they are not too busy. I go to bed at 7.30 pm.

I get up at 5.30 am, light the fires, make tea for the servants and clean the stove. I must clean the doorstep and the brass on the door by 7.00 am. Then I help Cook in the kitchen. I clean pans and help with breakfast. Then I wash up and do the vegetables for lunch. After lunch, I do more washing up and clean the kitchen. I finish by 3 pm and help Cook to make the servants' tea. Then we get tea for the family and do more washing up. After 7 pm, I clean the kitchen and fetch wood and coal for the next day's fires. I go to bed at 10 pm.

• Fill in the timetable for each girl's day.

Time	Jane's day	Julia's day
5 am		
7 am		
9 am		
11 am		
1 pm		
3 pm		
5 pm		
7 pm		
9 pm		

• Imagine you are Julia or Jane.
• Describe what you feel about the other girl's day.

Teachers' note Begin the lesson by reminding the children about the Victorian class system and how it affected the lives of everyone, including children. Make sure they realise that the girls' timetables do not exactly tie in with the divisions on the timetable they are filling in.

Developing History
Ages 9–10
© A & C BLACK

Changing children's lives

Understand that the work of individuals can change an aspect of society

I'm Thomas Barnardo. I was born in 1845. I studied to be a doctor in London and also helped at a ragged school. I was horrified by the way the poor boys at the school lived. I decided to do something about it.

- **How would Dr Barnardo have described what he did and his main achievements?**

- **Write what he might have said.**

Visit
www.barnardos.org.uk
to help with your research.

The first thing _____

_____

_____

_____

_____

_____

_____

_____

_____

What are Barnardo's homes like today?

- **Discuss with a partner.**

Teachers' note The children will need books, CD-ROMs and Internet access for their research. Begin by giving the children a brief outline of Dr Barnardo's life (see page 5). You can download a photo of Dr Barnardo for display from website www.ict.oxon-lea.gov.uk/best_practice/unit_11Barnardos/Barnardo3.jpg.

Developing History Ages 9–10
© A & C BLACK

Caught

This picture shows a policeman and a school inspector making children go to school.

- **Link the speech bubbles to the right person.**

School's no use to poor people. No one in our family has ever gone to school.

It's not fair! I can't find work if I'm at school.

They have to go to school. It's the law.

They will learn to read and write at school, This will help them find work.

I know I will hate school.

• How do you think compulsory education would have affected the people in the picture?

• What do you think the artist of the picture thought about compulsory education?

• Explain your reasons.

Teachers' note Before beginning the activity, remind the children that the 1870 Education Act made it compulsory for children to go school until they were 10 years old and that school inspectors and the police were employed to make them go. Make sure they understand the term 'compulsory' as well as the term 'voluntary'. The speech bubbles that deal with the law and learning link to either adult. The remaining speech bubbles link to the children.

Developing History
Ages 9–10
© **A & C BLACK**

All change

- **With a partner, discuss the similarities and differences between the pictures.**
- **Complete the chart.**

Where are they working? Who are they working with?

Picture A, 1742

Picture B, 1842

Similarities	Differences

Now try this!

- **Write a leaflet explaining the benefits of one of these ways of making cloth.**

Teachers' note Before beginning the activity, discuss the domestic and factory systems (see page 5). Some similarities include producing cloth and female workers working together. Some differences are working at home versus working in the factory; families working together versus lots of people who are not related working together;, a male supervisor in the factory only; and no small children allowed in the factory.

Developing History Ages 9–10 © A & C BLACK

16

Happy holidays

Present appropriate material that shows understanding of the Victorian period

- ## Choose one of these Victorian holidays.

Hop-picking and sorting

Seaside holiday

- ## What can you find out about this holiday?
- ## Write another question on the notepad. Use books or the Internet to find the answers.

You may need extra paper.

Questions	Answers
Who went on this kind of holiday?	
Where did they go?	
How did they get there?	

Now try this!

- ## Write a postcard home using the information you discovered.
- ## Draw a picture for the front.

Teachers' note The children will need books, CD-ROMs and the Internet for their research. Remind them that that their pictures need to be just as accurate as their written descriptions. Hop-picking was a working-class holiday. It was hard work but still in the open air and in the country. Seaside holidays were for the middle and upper classes.

Developing History Ages 9–10 © **A & C BLACK**

Picture the past

- **Find a painting or a photo of Victorian people at the seaside.**
- **What does it tell you about their life?**
- **How does the picture compare to seaside holidays today?**
- **Make notes in the table.**

What are they wearing?

What are they doing?

Holidays in Victorian times	Holidays today

Now try this!

- **Choose one adult and one child from the picture.**
- **What do you think they are feeling? Write an explanation.**

Teachers' note You will need several pictures of the seaside in Victorian times for this activity. Make sure there are people, especially children, in the pictures. Begin the activity by working through one of the pictures with the whole class. Get the children to identify all the play and activities going on and to describe the clothes the children are wearing.

**Developing History
Ages 9–10**
© A & C BLACK

18

Different homes

Understand that there are many representations of the Victorian period

- **Read these quotes about health and hygiene in Victorian homes.**

The water in the ditch was watery mud. Drains and sewers emptied into it. It was the only water the people could drink or cook and wash with. We were taken to a house where a child had died of cholera. The people said they had to drink the water unless they could beg or steal cleaner water from somewhere else.

Henry Mayhew, a newspaper reporter visiting a poor home.

I can't remember when we didn't have water piped into the house for cooking, washing and drinking. The servants brought me hot water to wash in each morning and I had a bath once a week. We didn't drink water much, mostly milk or very milky tea. None of us children were ever sick, only colds and the usual childhood sicknesses. We only had the doctor out once that I remember, when my sister, Lucy, had measles badly.

Clara, a child in a rich home.

According to Henry Mayhew, was Victorian hygiene good or bad?

- **Write a summary giving your reasons.**
- **Then write a summary of Clara's view of Victorian hygiene.**
- **Imagine you have spoken to both Henry and Clara. What conclusions would you draw about Victorian hygiene?**

Write your summaries on a separate sheet of paper.

Now try this!

- **Imagine you are Henry Mayhew.**
- **Describe a visit to Clara's house.**

Teachers' note Remind the children that, in Victorian times, the standards of sanitation, health and hygiene were much lower than today. Make sure they appreciate there are different viewpoints and perspectives on any subject. The children should write their summaries on a separate sheet. As a follow-up activity, ask them to compare Victorian and modern health and hygiene standards. Today, diseases such as tuberculosis and MRSA are often in the news.

Developing History
Ages 9–10
© A & C BLACK

Using the census

Find out about the past from census returns

- **Complete the survey using the local census records you were given.**

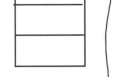

A household is everyone who lives in a house. People staying overnight were counted too.

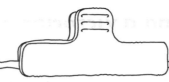

Local census survey

1. How many households are there?
2. How many of these are families?
3. How many people are in the largest family?
4. How many people are in the smallest family?

- **Choose a large household and fill in the report.**

Report on one family

1. Family surname _____
2. How old is the father? _____
3. How old is the mother? _____
4. How old are the children? _____
5. How many of the children work? _____
6. What does this suggest about the class of the family?

_____

- **With a partner, discuss who might not be counted in the census.**

Now try this!

- **Do all the heads of the household have a similar occupation?**
- **What does this tell you about the area they live in?**

Teachers' note The children will need local census sheets for this activity. Allow enough time to remind the children what a census is and introduce the pages you are using. Make sure they understand the following words and phrases before they begin the activity: census, occupation, household, head of household.

Developing History
Ages 9–10
© A & C BLACK

Full steam ahead

Make comparisons that illustrate changes in the Victorian period

- **Working with a partner, discuss how rail travel grew during Victorian times.**
- **Use the maps below and a Victorian map of your local area to help you.**

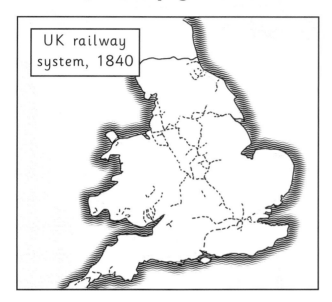

UK railway system, 1840

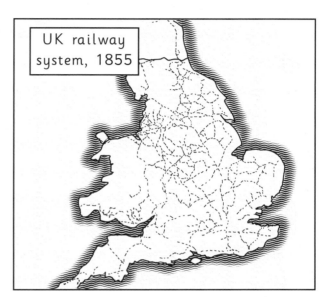

UK railway system, 1855

- **Complete this paragraph.**

Between 1840 and 1855 railways _____. There
were _____ lines in 1855. The nearest railway station to
my school in Victorian times was _____.
It is _____ away from where I live. I think it was
built there because _____
_____. The other ways you could travel
locally were _____ .

- **Discuss why you think rail travel grew so much.**

Now try this!

- **List four reasons for wanting a railway station in your town.**
- **List four reasons against the idea.**

Teachers' note You will need a map of your area from Victorian times showing the nearest railway station. A couple of reasons for rapid railway expansion are 1) the speed and efficiency of train travel compared to the transport of passengers and goods over roads and canals, and 2) the increased distance that people can travel to work and trade.

Developing History
Ages 9–10
© **A & C BLACK**

21

All aboard

The picture shows the three different boxed: classes of carriages on a Victorian train.

- **What are the differences between each class?**

Think about how crowded each carriage is.

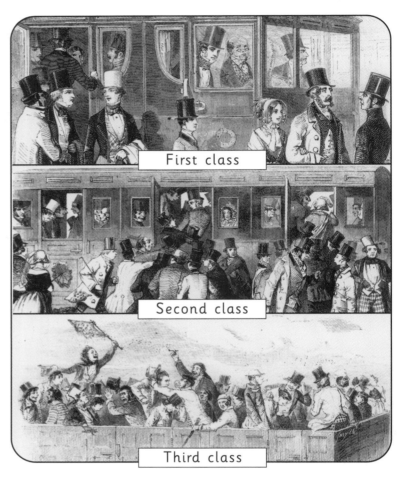

First class

Second class

Third class

- **Make notes on a chart like this.**

Class	Carriage features	Passengers
First		
Second		
Third		

- **In pairs, discuss the differences from rail travel today. What are the similarities?**

Now try this!

- **Write a diary entry for someone travelling in one of the carriages.**

Teachers' note Begin the lesson by reminding the children about the class system in Victorian Britain. Tell them to think about the way the carriages were made, how full they were and the kinds of people in them. First-class carriages were enclosed, had seats, curtains, privacy and space. Second-class carriages were enclosed with seats but were crowded. Third-class carriages were wooden boxes with no roofs. They had bench seats and were very crowded.

Developing History Ages 9–10
© A & C BLACK

Let's go shopping

Make comparisons that illustrate changes in the Victorian period

- **Look at photos of a shopping street taken at different years of the Victorian period.**

  What changes in the street do the latest photos show?

Do the shops look the same as before?

Are the people using the same types of transport?

Do the shops sell the same kind of things as they used to?

How much busier does the street look?

- **Write a report about the changes.**

- **Explain why you think they have happened.**

Name of street and town: _____

Dates of the photos: _____

_____

_____

_____

_____

_____

Now try this!

- **List any shops in a modern shopping street that are not in the Victorian photographs.**

Teachers' note The children will need several photos of a Victorian street to choose from. Your local library may have a collection of appropriate photos or there may be some on your council website. Make sure the children select photos from around 1840 and 1900 for the same street. You can make the follow-up work a class activity by asking the children to combine their answers. You could also arrange to take the children on a visit to a local Victorian museum.

Developing History
Ages 9–10
© A & C BLACK

Changing places

What evidence of Victorian times remains in a local area

- **Look at these views of a Victorian street.**

1840

1900

- **Circle the differences in the buildings and transport.**
- **How do you think the changes improved everyday life?**

_____

_____

_____

_____

_____

- **Compare pictures of a local street in Victorian times and the same street now.**

- **Write about the similarities and differences.**

Developing Histor
Ages 9–10
© **A & C BLACK**

Keep in touch

Analyse a change that occurred in Britain since 1948 and the reasons for it

In which decades were these ways of communicating in use?

- **Tick the boxes.**

> Some have been used for many decades.

Way of communicating	1950s	1960s	1970s	1980s	1990s	2000s
Telephone						
Letter						
Telegram						
Mobile phone						
Email						

- **With a partner, discuss the methods of communication. How did each of them improve communication?**

- **List the advantages and disadvantages of one of the methods.**

Advantages	Disadvantages
_____	_____
_____	_____
_____	_____
_____	_____
_____	_____

Is email a good way of keeping in touch?

- **Prepare an article for the Internet giving your opinion.**

Teachers' note Before beginning the activity, discuss the different methods of communication. Explain how some methods relay messages in days or weeks while others take a matter of seconds. The children can write their views about email on paper or a computer. If you have a school intranet, post the best reports on the site. The telephone, telegram and letter apply to all decades. The mobile phone and email have significant levels of use in the 1980s.

Developing History
Ages 9–10
© A & C BLACK

Going decimal

Up until 1971, Britain used old money such as shillings and crowns.

Then new money, called decimal currency, was introduced.

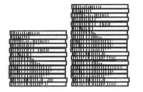

- Decide on the fewest coins you need for each amount in old money.

- Convert the amounts from old to new money.

- Use the conversion calculator to help.

CONVERSION CALCULATOR

Old money coins	Amount	Amount in new money
Halfpenny	1/2d	0.2p
Penny	1d	0.4p
Sixpence	6d	2.5p
Shilling	1s	5p
Crown	5s	25p
Sovereign	£1	£1

Old money	Coins needed	Amount in new money
£1 10s	1 sovereign, 2 crowns	£1.50
4s		
£3 7s		
9d		
11 1/2d		
£4 6s 8d		

Did all the old money convert exactly into new money?

- Explain what you think shopkeepers did if this did not happen.

Write on a separate sheet.

- Make up some conversions for the person sitting next to you.

- Make sure you know the answers before you check theirs.

Now try this!

Teachers' note Make sure the children understand how old money worked, with pounds, shillings and pence. The letter 'd' for pence comes from the small Roman coin of low value called a denarius. A chart of currency conversions for the wall would be useful for this activity. In the conversion calculator, the value of the new money conversion for the halfpenny and penny have been rounded down.

Developing History
Ages 9–10
© A & C BLACK

Clean and dry

Analyse a change that occurred in Britain since 1948 and the reasons for it

- **Cut out the cards.**
- **Label them using the word bank.**
- **Make a timeline from 1950 to 2000.**
- **Fix each card on the timeline to show when the item was mostly used.**

Use a separate sheet of paper to make the timeline.

Word bank

mangle
copper
twin tub
automatic washing machine
airer
tumble drier
washing line
hand washing

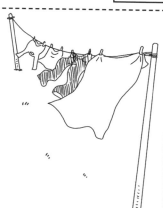

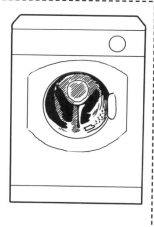

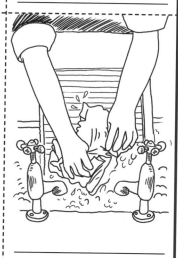

- **Write a description of how a 1950s housewife would hand-wash and dry dirty clothes.**

Teachers' note Discuss the word bank before beginning the activity. Make sure the children realise that soap powder and automatic washing machines are relatively recent inventions. Handwashing and line drying could be done in every period but they were mostly used in the 1940s and 1950s. The copper and mangle were also used in the 1940s and 1950s, the twin tub and spin dryer in the 1960s, and the automatic washing machine and tumble drier from the 1970s onwards.

Developing History
Ages 9–10
© **A & C BLACK**

Going to Butlins

Analyse a change that occurred in Britain since 1948 and the reasons for it

- **With a partner, choose one of the Butlins' holiday camps.**
- **Find out what it was like in the 1950s and 1990s.**
- **Fill in the table.**

You can find out lots of information at www.butlinsmemories.com

	1950s	1990s
Activities		
Rooms		
Food/meals		
Entertainment		

- **Imagine you stayed at the camp in 1950.**
- **Write a postcard to a friend about your holiday.**

Now try this!

- **How do you think the camp may have changed since 1990?**
- **Write an email about it to your friend.**

Teachers' note Children will need modern holiday brochures and information about Butlins for this activity. They can get the information from the Butlins website. Provide the children with small blank cards so they can make their own postcard or ask them to draw a postcard on a separate piece of paper or on the back of the activity sheet.

Developing History
Ages 9–10
© A & C BLACK

A person's history

Understand how personal memories can be used to find out about the past

- **Joan Shuter was interviewed about her life and work in the 1950s.**

"After the war, my husband and I went to live in Kent. I got a job in the local hospital, arranging care for patients when they left hospital. Then, in 1954, I became pregnant. Most married women stopped work to have children because the home and family became their job. Some women carried on working but only if their families needed the money badly. I gave up work. Then my husband decided to give up his job and buy a newsagent's shop. We ran that together because working in the shop did not interfere with looking after our home (in the flat over the shop) and our son, Paul. I had one other friend who also worked in a family business, a flower shop. All my other friends did not go to work. One or two of them stopped work as soon as they got married.

- **List three things about women and work that are different now.**

1. _____
2. _____
3. _____

- **List three things that are the same now.**

1. _____
2. _____
3. _____

- **Write why you think it was easier for Joan to work in the newsagents than going back to work at the hospital.**

Teachers' note Before beginning the activity, make sure children understand what oral history is. Differences for women today include going back to work after having children; working in many more kinds of occupations; and having babies later in life. Similarities include many women still having babies; children interrupting their parents' working lives; women working and bringing up families in family businesses; and women choosing to stop work to bring up their children.

Developing History
Ages 9–10
© A & C BLACK

Evidence

- **Match each piece of evidence to a decade.**

(1950s)   (1960s)   (1970s)   (1980s)   (1990s)

- **With a partner, choose one of the pieces of evidence.**
- **Discuss who might have used it.**
- **Write a description of the person.**

Find out on the Internet about other evidence from the Post-war Era, the Swinging Sixties and the Electronic Age.

_____

_____

_____

_____

_____

Now try this!

- **Choose a piece of evidence you think represents the 2000s for you.**
- **Make notes on why you chose it.**

Teachers' note Make sure that the children realise the electronic gadgets they have grown up with are modern inventions. Discuss how their parents didn't have these gadgets and wouldn't have been able to imagine that such things existed. The ration book links to the 1950s, the Beatles LP to the 1960s, the coat to the 1970s, the Walkman to the 1980s and the Megadrive to the 1990s.

Developing History
Ages 9–10
© **A & C BLACK**

30

Greek women

Consider some of the ideas of people living in Athens and Sparta

- **Imagine you are a time-traveller to ancient Greece.**
- **You visit Athens and Sparta and meet women there.**
- **Read what they tell you.**

I'm 30 and married with six children. I had three more girls, but the men decided not to keep them and killed them. I shop and run our home and estate. My husband lives in the barracks.

Hecabe, Sparta

I'm 19 and married with a baby boy. He will be a warrior like his father. Spartans aren't businessmen. My husband lives in the barracks, that's the law here. I spend a lot of time outdoors, exercising to stay fit to have more healthy babies

Xanthe, Sparta

I'm 18 and married with two babies. I spend most of my time in the women's rooms at home, making cloth and looking after the children. I run the home but can't deal with money. My husband or a slave does the shopping.

Agariste, Athens

I'm 30, with four children. I don't go out much. My husband died, so my father is looking for a new husband for me. I can't run the family business because I'm a woman.

Alcestes, Athens

- **Write a report for your guidebook like this.**

	Similarities	Differences
Work		
Family		
Business		
Money		

Now try this!

- **Imagine you are a Spartan woman visiting Athens.**
- **Write a letter home about attitudes to women in Athens.**

Teachers' note Remind the children about Greek city states and the importance of Athens and Sparta before they start the activity. Similarities between the women include being expected to marry, have babies and run the home. Differences include Athenians staying inside the home and not being allowed to handle money or run a business, and Spartans going out to exercise and do the shopping.

Developing History
Ages 9–10
© **A & C BLACK**

31

Democracy

Understand what is meant by democracy

- **Colour in green the statements that apply to an Athenian democracy.**
- **Colour in red the statements that do not.**

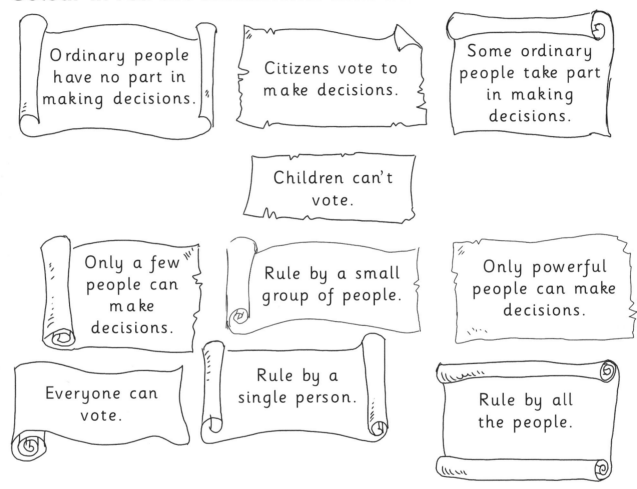

Ordinary people have no part in making decisions.

Citizens vote to make decisions.

Some ordinary people take part in making decisions.

Children can't vote.

Only a few people can make decisions.

Rule by a small group of people.

Only powerful people can make decisions.

Everyone can vote.

Rule by a single person.

Rule by all the people.

- **Design a poster to convince all the city states to become democracies.**

Women, children, slaves, and men who were not citizens **could not vote in Athens.**

- **Give two reasons why this is not 'government by the people'?**
- **Why do you think it was not practical to ask everyone about every decision?**

Teachers' note Before beginning the activity, discuss different forms of government. If your school or class has a council, look at ways in which council members are chosen. The statements that apply to an Athenian democracy are 'Some ordinary people take part in making decisions' and 'Citizens vote to make decisions'. The other statements do not apply.

**Developing History
Ages 9–10**
© **A & C BLACK**

Powerful gods

Learn about the beliefs of the ancient Greeks

- **Match the Greek gods and goddesses to the parts of life they controlled.**

Use books and the Internet to help you.

Zeus	the sea
Hera	weather and the other gods
Poseidon	fire and metalworking
Hades	hunting and children
Aphrodite	the underworld and wealth
Hesta	thieves and business
Ares	war
Apollo	love and beauty
Artemis	the home
Athena	marriage
Hermes	music
Hephaistos	cities, farming and work

Zeus

Athena

Apollo

Artemis

- **Who would you pray to if:**

you were in a bad storm at sea? _____

you were getting married? _____

you wanted your farm to make a lot of money?

_____

Now try this!

- **Find out how these gods and goddesses were related to each other.**
- **Draw a family tree.**

Teachers' note The children should have some prior knowledge of ancient Greek gods. Depending on work done previously, they may need research material or they can search for themselves on the Internet. The gods and goddesses link as follows: Zeus to weather; Hera to marriage; Poseidon to the sea; Hades to the underworld; Aphrodite to love; Hesta to home; Ares to war; Apollo to music; Artemis to hunting; Athena to cities; Hermes to thieves; Hephaistos to fire.

Developing History
Ages 9–10
© **A & C BLACK**

Towering temples

Make deductions about the Greek way of life from buildings

- **Label the Greek temple using the word bank.**

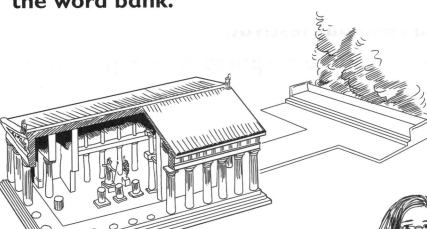

Word bank

altar
naos
front porch
back porch
columns
statue of the god
or goddess

Use books, CD-ROMs and the Internet to find out.

1. What were temples made from? _____

   _____

2. Who lived in them? _____

   _____

3. What were ordinary homes made from? _____

   _____

4. Who lived in them? _____

   _____

- **Discuss with a partner what your answers tell you about Greek religion.**

Now try this!

- **Imagine you are a Greek person trying to raise money to build a temple.**
- **Write a speech persuading people to give you the money.**

Teachers' note Before beginning the activity, work through the word bank with the children. Ensure they understand that 'naos' is a Greek word for the temple's inner room, or shrine room. Temples were made of stone for the gods to live in. Homes were made of mud brick for ordinary people to live in. The stone buildings have lasted and we can see some of them today, but the mud-brick homes have not.

Developing History
Ages 9–10
© A & C BLACK

34

Solve Sparta's problem

Understand the main characters in a famous battle

In 490 BC, the Persians invaded Greece. The Athenians asked the Spartans for help but the Spartans were in the middle of a 15-day religious festival.

- **Discuss the problem facing the Spartans with your group. Should they help or not?**

> Why should we help the Athenians? We are often at war with them! Let the Persians kill them.

> Perhaps the Athenians will beat the Persians on their own. They are good warriors.

> The Athenians can't win alone. There are 25,000 Persians. The Athenians only have about 10,000 men.

> The Persians are a greater enemy than Athens. City states should help each other in times like these.

> This is one of our most important religious festivals. The gods will be angry if we do not celebrate it properly.

> We will look like cowards if we do not go. Surely the gods will forgive us for ending the festival now to fight the Persians.

- **List three decisions they could make.**

1. _____

2. _____

3. _____

- **Imagine the Spartans decided not to help.**
- **Discuss how the Athenians would react to this news.**

Teachers' note Remind the children they need to think like Spartans, not like themselves, to do the activity. Ask each group for their decisions and talk about them. Then get the whole class to make a final vote. Afterwards, discuss what actually happened. The Spartans did not offer to help the Athenians until the festival was over but, by then, it was too late. Despite this, and against all the odds, the Athenians defeated the Persians at the Battle of Marathon in 490 BC.

Developing History
Ages 9–10
© A & C BLACK

Wonderful warriors

Infer information about Greek warfare

The phalanx

Greek warriors fought in a phalanx. They moved forwards and fought in rows, with their shields overlapping. The front row attacked the enemy with spears, then swords. If a warrior in the front row was killed, the man behind him stepped into his place.

- **Describe the strengths and weaknesses of a** | phalanx |.
- **Use the information to help you.**

The best thing a man can do for his city and his people is to stand firm in the front row of the phalanx. He should not think of running away, and should encourage the man beside him to stand firm, too.
Written around 650 BC by Tyrtaeus, a Spartan

Write your description on a separate piece of paper.

Now try this!

- **What would be the biggest problem for a phalanx once some members were killed?**
- **Explain your answer.**

Teachers' note Depending on the amount of experience the children have, the discussion of the evidence can be done as a whole class activity. A phalanx was hard to break through and gave the Greek soldiers very good protection. However, it relied on people not breaking the phalanx. It was difficult to keep a phalanx together on hilly ground or if there were lots of dead bodies to march over.

Developing History
Ages 9–10
© **A & C BLACK**

Olympic Games

Appreciate the range of sources of information about the ancient Greeks

- **Find a picture of a Greek vase showing an Olympic event.**
- **Complete the sentences.**

This vase shows a _____

event from the ancient Olympics. It tells me _____

_____

and _____.

It is an ancient Greek vase, so it is a _____

source for Greek Olympic events. An example of a secondary

source would be _____.

> Aren't you scorched by the sun? Aren't you cramped and crowded? Aren't the washing facilities bad? Aren't you soaked to the skin when it rains? Don't you get fed up with all the noise, the shoving and the other annoyances? But I think you are willing to put up with all of this for the marvellous spectacle.
>
> *Written by Epiktetus, a Greek thinker, about the Olympic Games*

- **Who at the Olympic Games is this written primary source describing?**

_____

- **Give your reasons for your answer.**

_____

_____

- **Using the sources to help you, draw a vase design that shows spectators at the Olympic Games.**

Teachers' note Remind the children of the difference between a primary and a secondary source. They will need images of Greek pots showing Olympic events. These can be found in books or on the Internet. The written source is describing the spectators.

Developing History
Ages 9–10
© **A & C BLACK**

Easy as ABC

- **The key compares the Greek alphabet with the English alphabet.**

Greek	α	β	γ	δ	ε	ζ	η	θ	ι	κ	λ	μ
English	a	b	g	d	e	z	–	–	i	k	l	m

Greek	ν	ξ	ο	π	ρ	σ	τ	υ	φ	χ	ψ	ϖ
English	n	x	o	p	r	s	t	u	–	–	–	–

How many Greek letters are there? _____

How many English letters are there? _____

Which English letters do not have Greek equivalents?

_____

Which English letters look similar to Greek letters?

_____

- **Using a dictionary, find two definitions of the Greek words** alpha **and** delta.

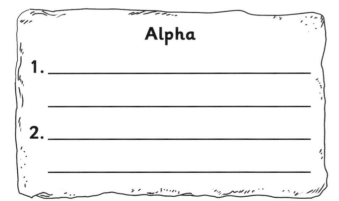

Alpha

1. _____

_____

2. _____

_____

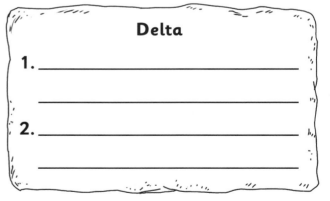

Delta

1. _____

_____

2. _____

_____

Now try this!

- **Find the names of all the letters of the Greek alphabet.**
- **Write them in order.**

Use the Internet to help you.

Teachers' note Explain to the children that they need to use the key to help them find the similarities and differences between the Greek and English alphabets. Make sure everyone understands these differences. Point out that the key shows the lower case versions of the Greek and English letters. The Greek alphabet has capital letters, too. You can find all the names of the letters at http://www.ibiblio.org/koine/greek/lessons/alphabet.html

Developing History
Ages 9–10
© A & C BLACK

School time

Consider why school life was different in ancient Greece

- **Compare your school life with the life of school boys in ancient Greece.**

- **Make notes in the table.**

Each of us has a slave to take us to school, carry our books and supervise our work. We can take our pets to school.

Boys aged 7-14 go to school if their parents can pay. Girls don't go to school. We have lessons in the morning and wrestling school in the afternoon. There are no school terms but we get religious festivals off.

There are only a few boys in each school. We learn altogether, in one room. We learn to read, write and do maths. Then we learn to sing and memorise poetry.

School today	School in ancient Greece

- **Work with a partner.**

- **Discuss the similarities and differences.**

- **What do you think are the reasons for the differences?**

- **Write a survival guide for a modern child going to a Greek school.**

- **Tell them what will be different.**

Teachers' note Remind the children before they start the activity to look out for similarities with and differences from modern schools. Similarities include learning to read and write, doing maths, and going to a school building with a teacher. Differences include only boys going to school, paying fees, singing in some lessons, smaller schools, taking slaves and pets to school, only having lessons in the morning, wrestling in the afternoon and no school terms.

**Developing History
Ages 9–10**
© A & C BLACK

Greek style

This is the Theatre Royal in London. It was built in 1819.

The building was designed in the boxed:classical **style of ancient Greece.**

- **Label the classical features.**

Word bank
column
pediment
capital
base
architrave

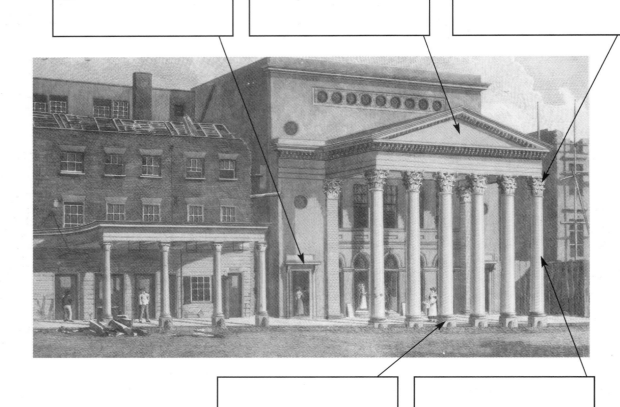

- **Imagine you are the architect who designed the building. Write a letter explaining why you chose this style of building.**

- **Design your own building using Greek architectural features.**

Teachers' note Make sure the children understand the words in the word bank before they start the activity. Show them pictures of classical buildings and point out the key features. Tell them to write the letter on the back of the activity sheet and to use the words describing architectural features that they have learned.

Developing History
Ages 9–10
© A & C BLACK

Greek thinkers

Recognise contributions made by ancient Greek scholars to our knowledge

- **Cut out the cards.**
- **Use books, CD-ROMs and the Internet to find out about each speaker.**
- **Match each thinker to their most famous area of study.**

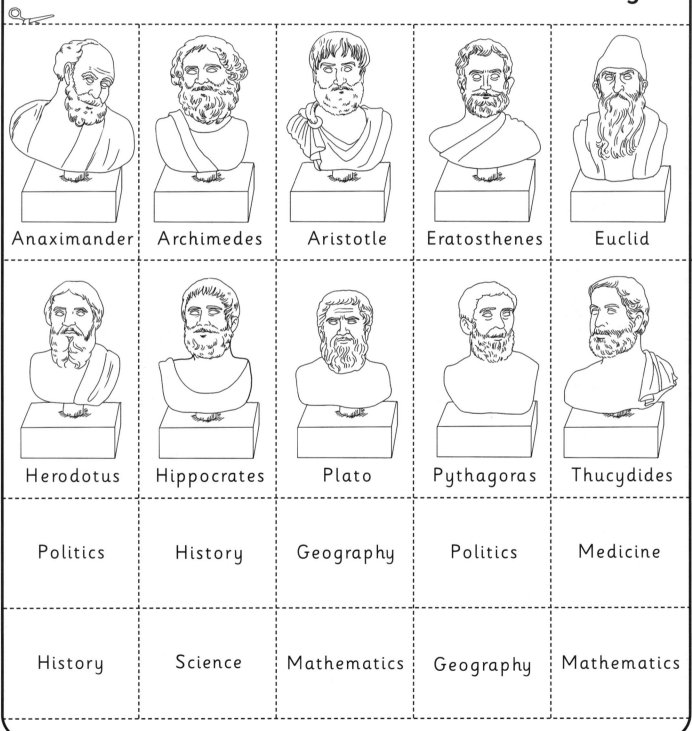

Anaximander	Archimedes	Aristotle	Eratosthenes	Euclid
Herodotus	Hippocrates	Plato	Pythagoras	Thucydides
Politics	History	Geography	Politics	Medicine
History	Science	Mathematics	Geography	Mathematics

Teachers' note These cards are designed to support the research work suggested in the QCA Schemes of Work for this unit. The cards match as follows: Anaximander to geography; Archimedes to science; Aristotle to politics; Eratosthenes to geography; Euclid to maths; Herodotus to history; Hippocrates to medicine; Plato to politics; Pythagoras to maths; Thucydides to history.

Developing History
Ages 9–10
© A & C BLACK

Olympics: 1

Compare the ancient and modern Olympics

They are held every four years in different parts of the world. Some professionals can compete in some of the newer events.

Our Olympics last for two weeks. People from all faiths compete.

The winner of each event is given a gold medal. The runners-up receive silver and bronze medals.

Our Olympics have hundreds of events for men and women. Anyone who can afford a ticket can watch.

The Olympics last for five days. No professionals can compete in our Olympics.

Our Olympics are a religious festival for Zeus. They are held every four years, always at Olympia.

Our Olympics began with just one event but now we have twelve. Only men can compete and watch. The athletes compete naked.

The winner of an event is given a laurel wreath and jars of olive oil.

Teachers' note You will need this information sheet and the activity sheet on page 43 to complete the activity.

Developing History
Ages 9–10
© A & C BLACK

42

Olympics: 2

Compare the ancient and modern Olympics

- **Compare the ancient and modern Olympics.**
- **Complete the table using the information from sheet 1.**

Similarities	Differences

- **Think of a modern Olympic event that could not have taken place at the ancient Greek Olympics.**
- **Explain why not.**

_____

_____

_____

What do you think is the most surprising difference between the Olympics then and now?
- **Give reasons for your choice.**

eachers' note Use this activity sheet together with the information sheet on page 42. Some examples of modern ents with equipment that was not available at the ancient Greek Olympics are shooting, cycling and archery. Another ew event is the marathon. There were no women's events at the ancient Greek Olympics.

Developing History
Ages 9–10
© A & C BLACK

Archaeological evidence

Know that Indus Valley cities shared some features

Archaeologist's notes about two Indus Valley cities

The bricks used to build the cities were all exactly the same size.

The cities were divided into an upper town and a lower town.

The upper town had bigger buildings in all the cities.

Both parts had walls around them.

The cities both had a complicated system of drains.

They both had lots of wells with fresh water.

Weights for weighing food have been found. They all use the same system.

Pottery with the same shapes and patterns have been found in both the cities.

Pottery figures with similar flattened faces and bodies have also been found.

- **Write a report about the cities using the archaeologist's notes.**

- **Explain if you think the cities all came from the same civilisation.**

  Which evidence gives the strongest support for this idea?

Report

_____

_____

_____

_____

Now try this!

- **Which evidence gives the weakest support for the idea?**

- **How else could you explain it?**

Teachers' note Start with a discussion about historical evidence based on best guesses. The evidence here suggests the two cities belonged to one civilisation because they shared many of the same features such as drains, bricks, and being divided into an upper and lower town. As people also used the same weights and measures, and made similar terracotta figures, this notion becomes even more likely. However, with no written evidence you cannot be completely sure.

Developing History
Ages 9–10
© **A & C BLACK**

Indus Valley homes

Know how people lived in Mohenjo Daro

- **Look at archaeological evidence in this modern drawing of an Indus Valley house.**

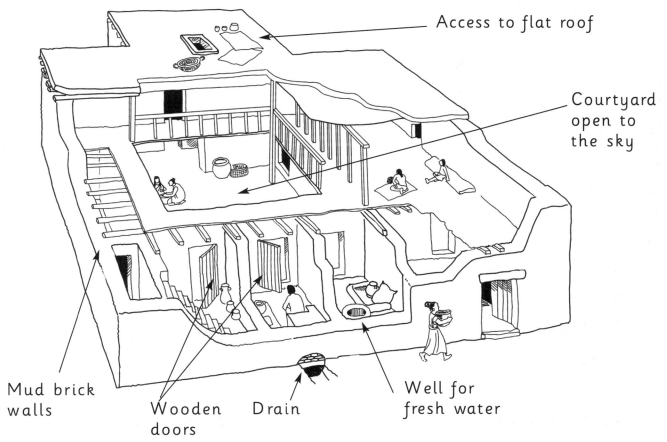

Access to flat roof

Courtyard open to the sky

Mud brick walls

Wooden doors

Drain

Well for fresh water

- **Fill in a chart like this.**
- **What does the drawing suggest about the climate in the Indus Valley?**
- **Explain your answer.**

Topic	What you can tell
Building materials	
Hygiene	
Water supply	

Now try this!

- **Write a survival guide for a modern child going to stay in an Indus Valley home.**
- **Explain what will be different.**

Teachers' note Make sure the children understand that the drawing is based on archaeological evidence and that they should look for inferences as well as facts. The facts are that the house has a flat roof, few windows and is built of mud brick. You can infer there was a good supply of water because the house has a drain and a well. The climate was probably dry. You can infer this because the roof is flat with a hole in it, which suggests that it did not rain much.

Developing History
Ages 9–10
© **A & C BLACK**

Interpreting evidence

Use pictures of artefacts to find out about an aspect of life in Mohenjo Daro

- **Choose a photograph of an artefact.**
- **Complete the table.**

Questions	Answers
What is the artefact?	
What is it made from?	
What kind of person do you think made it?	
What kind of person do you think it was made for?	
What does it tell you about the civilisation you are studying?	

Now try this!

- **Draw a labelled diagram of the artefact.**
- **Discuss your artefact with a friend.**

Teachers' note When deciding who the artefact was made for, the children need to consider the materials used. Were they expensive or hard to get? They should also consider the level of skill needed to make the artefact. This can tell them if there was any specialisation. The artefact can also reveal social levels. For example, it would be unlikely for farmers to wear gold jewellery. The children can use extra copies of the activity sheet to describe additional artefacts.

Developing History
Ages 9–10
© A & C BLACK

Take a close look

This is an Indus Valley sculpture, seen from three different angles. Do you think it is a man or a woman?

- **Circle your choice.**

- **Explain your reasons.**

I think this is a statue of a woman/man, because _____

_____ .

I notice the person's hair and beard are _____ .

The person is wearing _____

_____

I think this person was probably a _____ because

_____

_____

_____ .

- **List five things you would want to know about the drawing of an artefact before using it as evidence.**

Teachers' note Remind the children to explain their views each time. The statue is a man because the face has a beard. Both the beard and hair are carefully cut and looked after. The man is wearing a decorated robe and jewellery. He is probably a ruler, a priest or another important person. We know this because he has well-kept hair and fine clothing, and because a statue has been made of him.

Developing History
Ages 9–10
© A & C BLACK

47

Floating farmland

Know about how the Aztec people lived

The Aztec people of Tenochtitlan grew crops on small raised islands called chinampas.

- **Write a report explaining how this type of farming worked.**

- **Use the diagram to help you.**

Think about how chinampa farming is different to farming on dry land.

Chinampa held in shape with reed mats fixed to poles.

Crops include maize, chillies, peppers and onions.

Tree roots hold chinampa together.

Mud from lake bottom used as soil.

Mats filled with reeds, branches and stones.

Report: Chinampa farming

_____

_____

_____

_____

_____

_____

Now try this!

- **List three problems with chinampa farming.**

- **Explain why these problems might occur.**

Teachers' note Use the illustration as a prompt to discuss chinampa farming. Make sure the children understand what the word means before they start the activity. Allow plenty of time for this. Problems with chinampa farming include the mats and posts rotting underwater and needing to be replaced, the need to regularly bring up mud from the lake bottom to keep the soil fertile, and having to travel to and from to the chinampas particularly at harvest time.

Developing History
Ages 9–10
© A & C BLACK

A splendid city

Know about how people lived in Tenochtitlan

- **Imagine you are an explorer.**
- **On a separate piece of paper, write a letter home describing the main square at Tenochtitlan.**
- **Mention the buildings, the people and what happened there.**

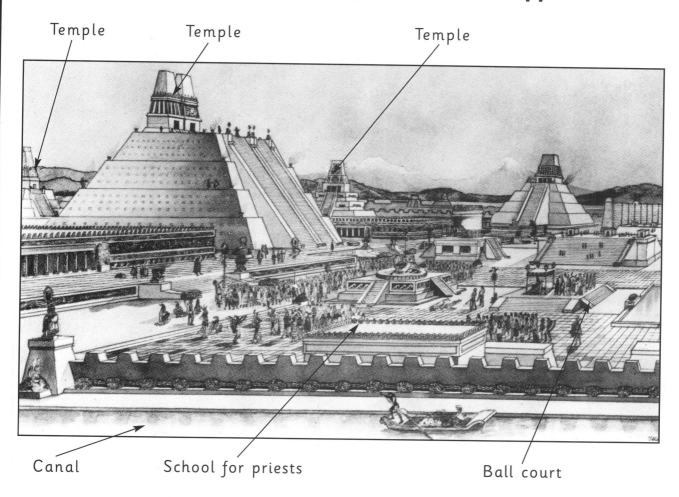

Temple   Temple   Temple

Canal   School for priests   Ball court

Drawing of the main square of Tenochtitlan, based on archaeological evidence. Everything in the main square was used for a religious ceremony.

Now try this!

- **Find a picture of the Acropolis in Athens. What was it used for?**
- **List similarities to and differences from the square at Tenochtitlan.**

Teachers' note Allow time for an introductory discussion using an enlarged version of the picture as a prompt. Make sure the children understand that the city was built in the middle of a large lake with the central part, including the main square, situated on a rocky island. For the similarities and differences between the Acropolis and the main square at Tenochtitlan, see page 10. Carry out this activity after the Floating farmland activity (page 48).

Developing History Ages 9–10 © A & C BLACK

Different views

Know that events can be interpreted in different ways

These people are discussing whether the Aztecs should have let the Spanish army into Tenochtitlan.

- **Join the speech bubbles to the most likely group of speakers.**

It was cowardly. Montezuma was scared.

It was the sensible thing to do. Cortez might have been the god, Quetzacoatl.

It made no difference. The Spanish would have won anyway.

The Aztecs are a peaceful people, not warriors.

It was right to give in. The Aztecs had no chance against the cannons and horses.

Montezuma may have thought that if he was friendly to the Spanish they would have made peace.

- **In pairs, discuss what advice you would have given Montezuma when the Spanish landed and why.**

Now try this!

- **Find out what happened to the Aztecs after Montezuma let the Spanish in.**
- **Use books, CD-ROMs and the Internet.**

Teachers' note Before the children begin the activity, tell the story of the Spanish arrival in Mexico. Ensure children understand which group are the Spanish people and which are the Aztecs. Some speech bubbles have a clear match. For example, only an Aztec will believe that Cortez might have been a god. Anyone might suggest that he was cowardly or that it was right to give in. This stresses the notion that points of view are subjective.

Developing History Ages 9–10
© A & C BLACK

Take a closer look

Use pictures to find out about aspects of Aztec life

These drawings are copies of Aztec drawings.

• **What do they tell you about Aztec family life?**

Picture	What can you see?	What does this tell you?

• **Write four adjectives to describe Aztec family life.**

_____ _____

_____ _____

What differences are there between Aztec family life and life today?

• **Discuss with a partner.**

Teachers' note Remind the children to think about what is happening, where and how. The drawings show you that fathers taught their sons while mothers taught their daughters. This tells you there was a division of labour between males and females. The males made boats, went fishing and built homes. The females prepared meals and wove cloth. The pictures also give information about clothes and cooking on open fires.

Developing History
Ages 9–10
© A & C BLACK

Tudor world view

Compare knowledge of the world between Tudor times and today

- **Use an atlas to mark the countries on the map.**

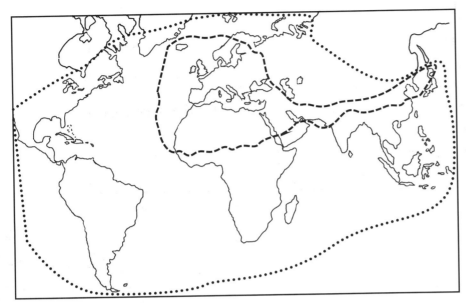

Word bank

Spain
France
England
India
China
Russia
Africa
North America
South America

Key

[dotted box] The world the Europeans knew in 1480

[dashed box] The world the Europeans knew in 1600

- **Name four parts of the world that were unknown in 1600.**

1. _____

2. _____

3. _____

4. _____

- **Imagine you are an explorer.**

- **Write to Queen Elizabeth asking for money to search for a new sea route to China.**

- **Explain why she should help you.**

Use a separate sheet of paper to write the letter.

Now try this!

- **Write Queen Elizabeth's reply.**

Teachers' note The children will need a modern atlas. Enlarge this page onto an A3 sheet of paper. Allow time at the start of the lesson for a short discussion about exploration. Reasons why the Queen might fund an expedition include to find new lands and claim them before someone else, and to make money from collecting spices, jewels and gold. Follow up the activity by asking the children to write poems about how sailors might have felt setting off into the unknown.

**Developing History
Ages 9–10**
© A & C BLACK

Life on board

Appreciate the discomforts of exploration

Golden Hind facts

People on board: 90
Toilets: none
Washing facilities: none
Beds: none except for the captain's
Kitchens: wood fire in a box of sand at the front of the ship
Food: live animals (chickens, goats), water, beer, oatmeal, beef in barrels of salt

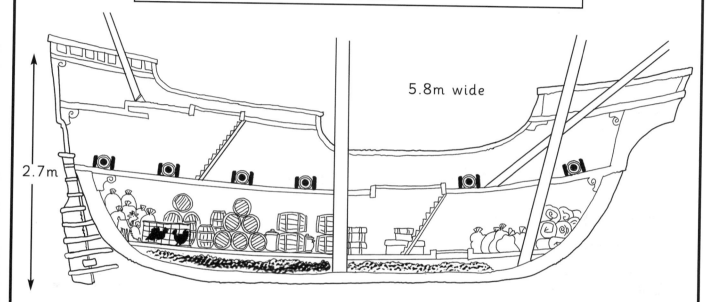

5.8m wide

2.7m

21.3m long

Imagine you are the new cabin boy on the Golden Hind.

- **Write a note to your parents describing the ship and what you are looking forward to on your trip.**

- **Use a separate piece of paper.**

- **Write a report about the food on the ship. What is missing for a healthy diet?**

Teachers' note The children may find it difficult to visualise the size of the Golden Hind, so for an extension activity, you mark out its actual size with chalk in the playground. There were about 90 people on board. Stand the class inside the outline. How many more children do you need to make up the numbers?

Developing History
Ages 9–10
© A & C BLACK

Dangerous voyages

Appreciate the discomforts of exploration

- **Play the game with a partner.**

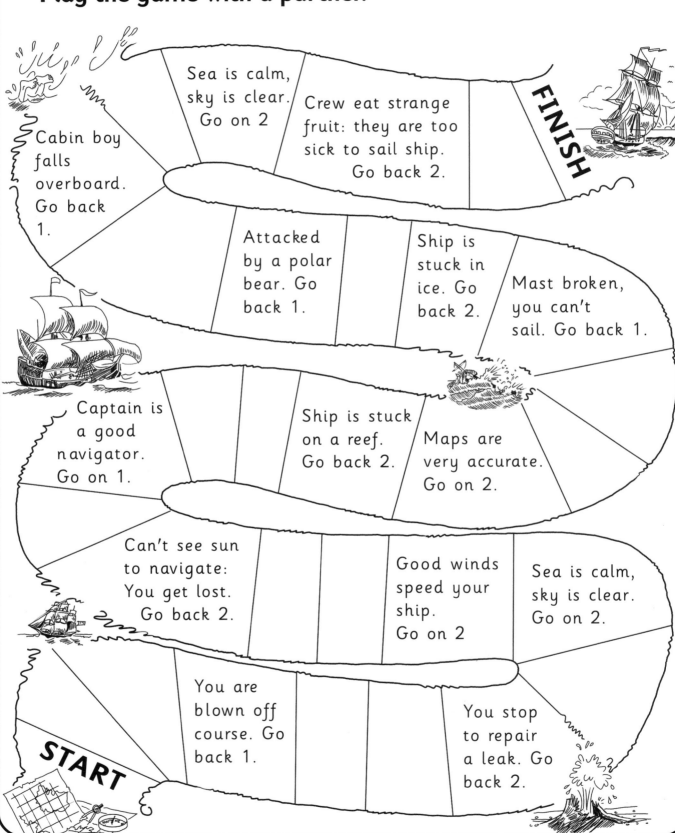

Sea is calm, sky is clear. Go on 2

Crew eat strange fruit: they are too sick to sail ship. Go back 2.

FINISH

Cabin boy falls overboard. Go back 1.

Attacked by a polar bear. Go back 1.

Ship is stuck in ice. Go back 2.

Mast broken, you can't sail. Go back 1.

Captain is a good navigator. Go on 1.

Ship is stuck on a reef. Go back 2.

Maps are very accurate. Go on 2.

Can't see sun to navigate: You get lost. Go back 2.

Good winds speed your ship. Go on 2

Sea is calm, sky is clear. Go on 2.

You are blown off course. Go back 1.

You stop to repair a leak. Go back 2.

START

Teachers' note Before beginning the game, remind the children about the dangers of overseas exploration. If the children have studied the topic before, brainstorm how the explorers navigated. If they have not, explain that navigation was done by the sun, moon and stars, or by landmarks. All these methods relied on clear weather. The children will need counters and a dice to play the game.

**Developing History
Ages 9–10**
© **A & C BLACK**

Round the world: 1

Apply chronology

- **Sort the cards into the correct order to chart Francis Drake's journey around the world from 1577 to 1580.**

27 Dec, 1577, arrive at Mogador. Repairs. Travel along coast and capture two Spanish ships.	Leave Plymouth again on 13 Dec with five ships (Pelican, Elizabeth, Swan and Christopher).	Finally reached the Philippines on 16 Oct, 1579. Have been sailing for over four months.
Leave Cape Verde on 2 Feb. Take captured ship, renamed the Mary.	Arrive at Cape Verde Islands on 28 Jan, 1578. Capture Portuguese ship and take its supplies.	3 Nov, 1579. Arrived at the Spice Islands. Take six tons of cloves on board.
26 Sept, 1580. Arrived finally at Plymouth with 58 men. Is the Queen still alive?	Set sail from Plymouth, UK on 15 Nov 1577 but return because winds are against us.	10 June, 1578, reach Port St Julian. Fighting with local people. Pelican renamed Golden Hind.
Reach Panama, South America, on 1 April. Claim the land and rename it New Albion.	Feb, 1579, raids on Arica in Chile and Callao. More Spanish ships captured.	Raid on Valparaiso, South America, on 5 Dec, 1578. We take gold and wine from a Spanish ship.
Reach Rio de la Plata, Brazil, on 16 April, 1578. Towns on the coast are Spanish and dangerous.	Leave Port St Julian. Pass through Straits of Magellan to Pacific Ocean. It is 6 Sept.	1 June, 1579. Have set sail north. Ship leaking badly. Decide to cross Pacific to get home.
Landed at Sierra Leone, 22 Jul, without stopping since Java. On the home stretch now.	30 Sept, 1578. Bad storms. Golden Hind blown 300 miles south to Cape Horn.	26 Mar, 1580. Arrived at Java but had to ditch three tons of cloves when we hit a reef.

Teachers' note You will need this information sheet and the activity sheet on page 56 to complete the activity. Before the children start, remind them of the circumstances surrounding Drake's voyage (see page 10).

**Developing History
Ages 9–10**
© A & C BLACK

Round the world: 2

Apply chronology

• Plot Francis Drake's journey around the world on the map.

Use the cards from Round the world: 1 to help you.

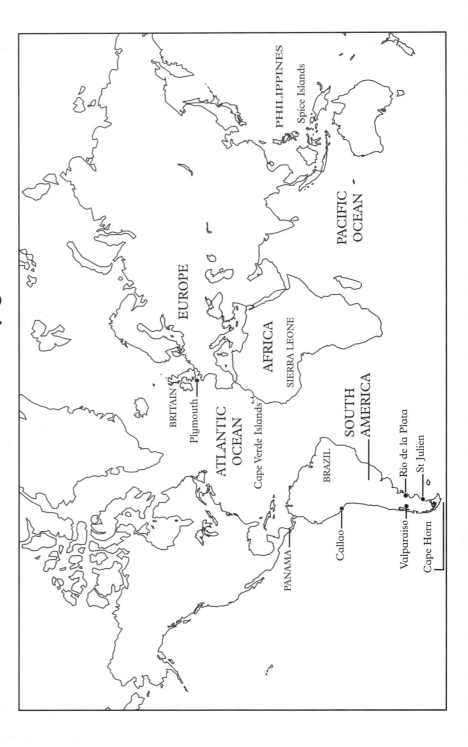

Teachers' note Use this activity sheet together with the information sheet on page 55. Remind the children of the circumstances surrounding Drake's voyage (see page 10) and explain what the word 'chronological' means. Blow up the map to A3 on a photocopier. The children will need atlases to help them. Get them to plot the route in pencil first, in case they make a mistake.

Developing History
Ages 9–10
©A & C BLACK

Viewpoints

- ## Underline the words that seem biased against the inhabitants.

Drake and eight of us sailed to land to look for supplies of fresh water. We landed and were greeted in a friendly way by two inhabitants of the place. They and Master Oliver competed at shooting arrows and he shot much further. Then a sour-looking person came and talked to them angrily, trying to turn them against us. Mr Robert Winter, thinking to amuse them as Mr Oliver, shot his bow but it broke. These treacherous fellows now thought they had the advantage of us, not realising our swords and guns were weapons. They waited until we (without suspecting evil) began to move to the boat, then fired arrows at us, wounding Mr Oliver and killing our master gunner as he fired at them. Drake told us to move about, to make harder targets for these monsters, and to break all their arrows that we could find so they could not use them again. I came close enough to get the gun and shot one of them dead. At this, they all ran away.

Francis Fletcher, who sailed on Drake's ship, said this about meeting local people when looking for water near St. Julien.

1. Who does Fletcher blame for the violence? _____

_____

2. Who does he sees as the hero of the escape?
Explain your reasons. _____

_____

_____

- ## Write a local person's biased version of what happened.

- ## Write an impartial account of what happened.

Now try this!

Teachers' note Make sure the children understand what the word 'bias' means before they begin the activity. Read through the quotation together as a class, first. Explain that Fletcher was the chaplain on the expedition, so he had the most time (and a good education) for recording the events. However, point out that just because he was a primary source for the event, this does not make him unbiased.

Developing History
Ages 9–10
© A & C BLACK

Different lives

Find out about the way of life of indigenous people before colonisation

- ## Work with a partner.
- ## Discuss the lives of the people living in the village.

Wooden frame for building

Wooden boards

Fence of poles

Entrance

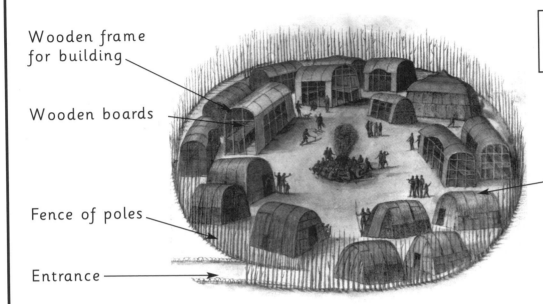

Pomeioc village, drawn by John White in 1584.

Woven mats to cover buildings

- ## Complete the chart.

Things we know	Things we think

Now try this!

What do you most want to know about the villagers?

- ## Write three questions.

Teachers' note Make sure the children understand the difference between the things they are sure of and guesses they make based on evidence. Remind them of the work they have done on facts and inferences and explain that this is the skill they are using to fill out the table. You can find examples of the 'things we know' and the 'things we think' in the notes on page 11.

Developing History Ages 9–10
© A & C BLACK

Exploration impact

Recall and summarise what has been learned about the effects of exploration

- ## Complete the speech bubbles.

All that exploring helped sailors and traders because

_____

Yes, and look at the new foods they brought back that we wouldn't want to do without now, such as

_____

_____

But they brought back stuff that is really bad for us, too. The most obvious one is

_____

Setting up colonies just led to trouble later. An example of this is

_____

_____

- ## Which of the effects above was most important?
- ## Explain your answer.

Now try this!

- ## Imagine you are having a traditional Christmas dinner and all the foods discovered by the Tudors have vanished.
- ## Describe the meal and how you feel about it.

Teachers' note Begin the lesson by discussing the effects of Tudor exploration. Brainstorm ideas and write them on the board. Remind the children to consider both good and bad effects, and whether they were intentional or unintentional. Discuss the fact that some changes are short-term or temporary, others long-term or permanent. Encourage the children to exchange ideas about changes that are taking place with modern exploration, such as space exploration.

Developing History
Ages 9–10
© **A & C BLACK**

Bob Geldof

Research the basic details of a person's life and present them chronologically

- **Plan a homepage for a website about Bob Geldof.**
- **Decide on the menu options, write about Bob Geldof's life, and add facts and pictures.**

☐ ☐ ☒

Welcome to my Bob Geldof website!

| Home |
| News |
| |
| |
| |

All about Bob

Bob Geldof was born in 1951…

Bob facts

1.

2.

3.

PHOTO
ALBUM

- **Write a letter to Bob Geldof.**
- **Explain what you admire about him most.**

Teachers' note The children will need research information and pictures for this activity. You can provide them with edited information from the websites listed on page 11. Before beginning, discuss the kinds of information that a website reader would want to find. Depending on the amount of Internet work done before, the children may need to begin by looking at some other home pages. This will require Internet access.

Developing History
Ages 9–10
© **A & C BLACK**

Band Aid

Give some reasons for celebrity involvement in aid work

- **Fill in the missing words using the word bank.**

Word bank		
music	Christmas	million
pop	Ethiopia	bands
solve	1984	

Band Aid was set up in _____ . Bob Geldof watched a programme about the famine in _____ . He got over 40 big _____ stars to make a record called 'Do they Know it's _____ ?' The record sales made over £8 _____ for famine relief. It was called Band Aid because _____ were sending aid to Africa. But a band aid is a kind of plaster. They were saying their money could not _____ the problem, but it was some help.

- **Why do you think Bob Geldof set up Band Aid?**
- **Why didn't he just give the money to charity?**

_____

_____

_____

_____

_____

Geldof said, "We make giving exciting."

- **Explain how you think he achieved this.**

Teachers' note Before the children start the activity, discuss how important motivation is in the study of history. Some reasons for Bob Geldof starting Band Aid include wanting to make a difference, wanting to get around all the red tape surrounding established charities, and wanting to focus on one place at one time (many charities tend to work worldwide). You can extend the activity with a discussion about Bob Geldof's importance to the whole project.

Developing History
Ages 9–10
© A & C BLACK

Making things happen

Compare primary and secondary sources available for the study of a person

What do these sources tell you about the impact of Band Aid?

- **Complete the sentences.**

Source A

Water and sanitation	£564,353
Health improvement	£1,910, 826
Food and security	£1,105,495
Education	£421,793
TOTAL	£4,002,467

Table showing how money raised by the Band Aid Charitable Trust was spent in 2005.

Source B

You can count the years since we first asked for your help in trees and dams and fields and cows and camels and trucks and schools and health clinics, medicines, tents, blankets, clothes, toys, ships, planes, tools, wheat, sorghum, beans, workshops. Maybe you should try to count the years in terms of people. There are thousands upon thousands of people in a bitter and blasted part of the planet who were helped.

Part of a letter from Bob Geldof on the Live Aid website.

Both sources tell me _____.

Source A tells me more about _____.

Source B tells me more about _____.

If I could only use one source to show the effects of Band Aid it would be source ____ because _____.

The primary source about Bob Geldof is _____.

It tells me he _____

_____

_____

- **Write the lyrics for a song about the effects of Band Aid.**

Teachers' note Begin by telling the children that they will be looking at two sources, both about the effects of the Band Aid Trust. Read the sources together and discuss the language used. Before they start the activity, discuss the differences between primary and secondary sources.

Developing History Ages 9–10
© A & C BLACK

More aid

Begin to evaluate the impact of an individual on the history of his time

- **Use the Internet to research what Bob Geldof and Band Aid did after raising money for Africa in 1984.**
- **Make notes in the table.**

Event	Date and place	What happened
Live Aid		
Sport Aid		
'Run the World'		
Band Aid II		
Band Aid 20		
Live 8		

- **Design a poster to advertise one of these charity events.**
- **Think of the best way to get your message across.**

Teachers' note Children will need access to books, CD-ROMs and the Internet for their research. Use the notes to discuss the increase in Geldof's political campaigning and how this can lead you to think that he believes the most effective method of making a difference is through political change.

Developing History
Ages 9–10
© **A & C BLACK**

Changing people

Band Aid starts in 1984

Comic Relief starts in 1985.

DATA (Debt, Aid, Trade for Africa) starts in 2002.

Live Aid, Sport Aid, Band Aid 11, Live 8 and Band Aid 20 follow.

Project Red starts in 2006. Well-known companies donate money from some of the products they sell.

Make Poverty History takes place in 2005. Large and small charities work together with celebrities.

What impact has Band Aid had on charity work?

How important do you think Bob Geldof and Band Aid are?

- **Write your answers on the notepad.**

_____

_____

_____

_____

_____

Now try this!

- **With a partner, discuss what you know about Comic Relief.**

- **List the similarities and differences to Band Aid.**

Teachers' note This activity can be done as a whole-class discussion. Before you begin, remind the children that historians often debate cause and effect as well as the level of responsibility of one person but these things are opinion. It is possible to argue that, without Bob Geldof, the change would not have happened. You could also argue that Bob Geldof reflected a change in the way people were thinking and that someone else would have done something similar.

Developing History
Ages 9–10
© A & C BLACK